Exotic
COOKERY

littlewoods

Series Editor: Stella Henvey
Series Art Director: Grahame Dudley
Photographer: Paul Kemp
Stylist: Jane Kemp
Home Economist: Moya Maynard

This edition first published for
The Littlewoods Organization plc in 1984 by
Orbis Publishing Limited, London

© 1984 Orbis Publishing Limited

Printed in Italy by Interlitho, Milan

NOTES

Imperial and metric measurements are not exact equivalents, so follow one set only. Graded measuring spoons are used. Measurements are level unless otherwise specified.

The oven should be preheated to the recommended temperature. Bake on the centre shelf unless otherwise directed.

To check the temperature of oil for deep frying without a thermometer, drop in a ½in/1cm bread cube, if the oil is the correct temperature (370F/185C) the bread will brown in 55 seconds.

Unless otherwise stated flour is white, oil is vegetable, herbs are fresh, vegetables and fruit are washed, trimmed and peeled; eggs are medium (EEC sizes 4-5).

CONTENTS

INTRODUCTION

If you have a taste for adventure, or simply want to spice up your cooking repertoire, you will find plenty of easy and exciting recipes in Exotic Cookery. Starting with the Orient, the chapters cover spicy Mexican and Caribbean food, aromatic Indian dishes plus mouthwatering meals from the Mediterranean and Middle East.

    The ingredients used in the recipes are available from good supermarkets or Asian and Continental food stores, so you can enjoy exotic food at home.

INGREDIENTS
Here are some items used in the recipes

1 A wok is a Chinese frying pan. A large thin frying pan is a good substitute.
2 Coriander leaves
3 Soy sauce: a salty flavouring widely used in Chinese cooking. Use light soy sauce in fish, chicken and vegetable dishes; rich soy sauce with meat.
4 Peppers are usually green or red, but yellow and black peppers are increasingly available. Cut off the tops and remove the seeds and membrane.
5 Chinese cabbage
6 Mange tout are eaten whole.
7 Mooli
8 Okra
9 Mangoes
10 Limes
11 Fresh beansprouts; rinse under cold running water before using
12 Long grain rice: use for pilafs and risottos.
13 Basmati rice, for Indian pilaus, must be cleaned before use: rinse in 6-7 changes of cold water, then cover with fresh water for 30 minutes and drain.
14 Turmeric
15 Ground cumin
16 Cumin seeds
17 Cloves
18 Green cardamom pods. White cardamom pods have been bleached. Black cardamom pods are larger, less expensive and less aromatic.
19 Sweet paprika
20 Cinnamon sticks
21 Ground coriander
22 Fresh rosemary
23 Fresh fennel
24 Fresh summer savory
25 Fresh sage
26 Fresh chives
27 Red lentils
28 Chana dal is sold in Indian and Pakistani food stores. Yellow split peas can be used instead.
29 Moong dal is sold in Asian and Greek supermarkets and some health food stores.
30 Chilli tassels make an attractive garnish for meat dishes. Use fresh chillies and cut off the tips, then scrape out the seeds. Slit each pod lengthways into strips, without cutting through the stem end.
31 Spring onion tassels make a delicate garnish for Chinese dishes. Choose onions with a thick stem

and slim bulb. Trim to 4-5in/
10-13cm long. Make 2-3 slits in
either end without cutting through
the the centre. Leave in iced water
for 1 hour to curl, then drain.
32 Egg noodles
33 Taco shells: spicy corn
pancakes, folded to hold a filling.
Sold in packets.
34 Tostadas: flat corn pancakes,
deep-fried until crisp. Sold in
packets.
35 Fresh and dried chillies. For a
less pungent flavour, cut the pods
open and discard the seeds. Wash
hands well after handling chillies.

36 Pine nuts
37 Fresh root ginger
38 Shelled peanuts
39 Unsalted cashew nuts
40 Garlic cloves
41 Chinese Five Spice Powder.
Sold in jars in supermarkets.
42 Red food colouring is sold in
Asian stores. It contains the dye
tartrazine which can cause an
allergic reaction.,
43 Black mustard seeds
44 Saffron strands. To grind, place
the strands in a small bowl and
grind to a fine powder with the end
of a rolling pin.

CHINA AND THE FAR EAST

SWEETCORN AND CRAB SOUP

6oz/170g can crabmeat, drained and flaked
1 egg white
1½ pints/850ml chicken stock
2x10½oz/290g cans creamed sweetcorn
3tbls cornflour
1tbl dry sherry
To garnish:
2oz/50g slice of ham, cut into thin shreds
coriander sprigs

Reserve a few pieces of crabmeat. Mix the rest with the egg white.

Pour the stock into a saucepan and bring to the boil, then stir in the sweetcorn.

Blend the cornflour with the sherry and 2tbls water. Stir in a little of the hot stock mixture, then pour into the pan. Cook, stirring, until the soup thickens and clears.

Using a fork, gradually stir in the crabmeat and egg-white mixture.

Ladle the soup into individual bowls. Garnish with the reserved crab pieces, shreds of ham and a sprig of coriander. Serve at once. **Serves 6-8**

WATERCRESS SOUP

1½ pints/850ml chicken stock
1tbl soy sauce
black pepper
1 bunch watercress, finely chopped
4 spring onions, thinly sliced
2oz/50g cooked chicken meat, finely shredded
1tsp sesame oil
salt

Pour the stock into a saucepan and bring to the boil. Add the soy sauce and a little pepper.

Add the watercress and bring back to the boil. Stir in the spring onions, chicken meat and oil. Season to taste and serve at once. **Serves 4-6**

PRAWN AND EGG SOUP

1 chicken stock cube
1 fish stock cube
6oz/175g peeled prawns,
  defrosted if frozen
1 egg, well beaten
2 spring onions, cut into
  short lengths

Heat 1½ pints/850ml water in a saucepan, add the stock cubes and stir until dissolved.

Reserve a few of the smaller prawns; chop the rest and add to the pan. Bring to the boil, then remove from the heat. Pour the beaten egg into the soup in a very thin stream, stirring constantly so that it sets in strands.

Return the pan to low heat, add the spring onions and heat through gently for a few seconds.

Ladle the soup into individual bowls. Garnish with the reserved prawns and serve at once. **Serves 4-6**

MUSHROOM SOUP

Place the consommé in a saucepan with ¾ pint/450ml water. Heat gently, stirring, until smoothly blended, then stir in the spring onions and sherry. Bring to the boil, add the mushrooms and ginger and cook gently for 5 minutes.

Stir in the chicken and heat through gently. Serve at once. **Serves 6-8**

2 x 10oz/275g cans condensed consommé
2 spring onions, thinly sliced
1 tbls sherry
4oz/100g button mushrooms, thinly sliced
4 thin slices fresh root ginger
2oz/50g cooked chicken meat, finely shredded

SPRING ROLLS

4oz/100g plain flour
2 eggs, beaten
¼ pint/150ml milk
1 tbls oil
oil, for frying
For the filling:
1 tsp salt
¼ tsp black pepper
¼ tsp cornflour
4oz/100g pork, cut into
   thin strips
2 tbls soy sauce
6 spring onions, chopped
4oz/100g carrots, cut into
   thin strips
4oz/100g bamboo shoots,
   cut into thin strips
4oz/100g beansprouts
6oz/175g peeled prawns,
   defrosted if frozen,
   chopped

Sift flour into a mixing bowl. Add eggs, milk, oil and 2½fl oz/65ml cold water. Beat to make a smooth batter.

Heat a little oil in a heavy-based 7in/18cm frying pan. Pour off the excess. Pour a little batter into the pan and swirl over the base, then cook over moderate to high heat until the underside is golden. Slide pancake on to greaseproof paper. Make 11 more pancakes, cooking each on 1 side only.

To make the filling, place salt, pepper, cornflour, pork and soy sauce in a bowl and mix well. Heat 4tbls oil in a wok or large frying pan. Add the pork and stir-fry over high heat for 30 seconds. Remove with a slotted spoon.

Add the onions and stir-fry for 2-3 seconds. Add the carrots, bamboo shoots, beansprouts and prawns, stir-frying each for a few seconds before the next addition. Remove from the heat and stir in pork. Allow to cool slightly.

Divide filling between the pancakes, placing it on the cooked side. Fold the sides over the filling, then roll up.

Heat a little oil in the pan. Fry the rolls, a few at a time, until crisp and golden. Drain and serve. **Makes 12**

GADO GADO

Prepare the sauce: dissolve the coconut in ½ pint/300ml warm water. Heat the oil in a saucepan, add the onion and garlic and fry until lightly browned. Remove from the heat and stir in the peanut butter, dissolved coconut, tamarind, sugar and salt to taste. Bring the sauce slowly to the boil and cook, stirring, for 2-3 minutes until thickened. Set aside to cool.

To make the salad, heat the oil in a frying pan. Add the onion rings and fry until browned; drain and reserve.

Cut the beans into ½in/1cm lengths and cook in boiling salted water for 2 minutes; drain and rinse under cold water.

To assemble, arrange the spinach over a serving dish and top with the beansprouts, carrots, cabbage, beans and rice. Spoon some of the peanut sauce on top and garnish with the browned onion rings. Serve remaining sauce separately. **Serves 4**
Note: Gado Gado, which means a mixture, is a very popular Indonesian salad. The ingredients can be varied but always include a combination of fresh salad and cooked vegetables.

For the peanut sauce:
2oz/50g creamed coconut
2tbls oil
1 onion, finely chopped
2 garlic cloves, crushed
6oz/175g crunchy peanut butter
1tsp tamarind extract
1tbls soft light brown sugar
salt
For the salad:
1-2tbls oil
1 small onion, sliced and separated into rings
4oz/100g French beans
4oz/100g spinach, shredded
2oz/50g beansprouts
4oz/100g carrots, coarsely grated
4oz/100g Chinese cabbage, shredded
4oz/100g cooked rice

FRIED RICE

2tbls oil
1 celery stalk, sliced
6oz/175g cooked rice
3 spring onions, chopped
1 egg
7oz/200g can peeled
  prawns, drained
4oz/100g ham, very
  thinly sliced
1tsp light soy sauce

Heat 1tbls oil in a wok or frying pan.
Add the celery and stir-fry for 1 minute.
Add the remaining oil. Add the rice
and stir-fry until just lightly browned.
Add the spring onions and stir-fry for
30 seconds. Make a well in the centre of
the mixture.

Beat the egg with 1tbls water and
pour into the well in a thin stream,
stirring constantly until lightly
scrambled.

Add the prawns, ham and soy sauce
and stir until heated through.

Serve at once. **Serves 4-6**

NOODLE NESTS

6oz/175g egg noodles
salt
5tbls oil
For the filling:
4oz/100g broccoli spears
4oz/100g chicken livers,
  sliced
1 garlic clove, crushed
2 spring onions, sliced
1/4tsp cornflour
1tbls sherry
2oz/50g ham, thinly sliced

Cook the noodles in boiling salted
water for 4-6 minutes, until just tender.
Drain well, place on absorbent paper
and separate into 4 equal round piles.

Heat 4tbls oil in a frying pan. Fry the
noodles, 2 piles at a time, over medium
heat for 1-2 minutes on each side until
crisp and browned. Use a fish slice to
draw the edges of the noodles towards
the centre to keep a rounded shape.
Transfer to a plate and keep warm.

Break the broccoli into florets and cook for 1 minute in boiling salted water, then drain well.

Heat remaining oil in pan. Add chicken livers, garlic, spring onions and broccoli. Blend cornflour with the sherry and stir into the pan with the ham. Stir-fry for 20-30 seconds, then divide between the nests and serve.
Serves 4

SPRING ONION PANCAKES

Sift flour into a bowl. Slowly stir in 4fl oz/120ml hot water; mix to a dough. Turn out on to a floured surface and knead briefly until smooth. Wrap in cling film and leave for 30 minutes.

Roll dough into a sausage shape about 2in/5cm thick and cut into 8 slices. Flatten each slice into a small round and make a shallow dent in the centre. Place a dot of lard and a little chopped spring onion in each dent. Fold the edges of the dough over the filling and pinch together to seal. Turn over so the seams are underneath, then roll out each pancake to a 3in/8cm circle.

Heat the oils together in a frying pan. Fry the pancakes gently, in batches, for 4 minutes, turning frequently. Garnish, and serve hot, with soy sauce. **Makes 8**

6oz/175g plain flour
1oz/25g lard
3tbls spring onions, finely chopped
½tsp salt
3tbls sesame oil
2tbls sunflower oil
spring onion tassels, to garnish (optional)
soy sauce, to serve

PORK AND PRAWN STIR-FRY

8oz/225g pork tenderloin
2tbls oil
1tsp sesame oil
4 thin slices fresh root
    ginger
8oz/225g can water
    chestnuts, drained and
    thinly sliced
½ small red pepper,
    seeded and thinly sliced
4oz/100g peeled prawns,
    defrosted if frozen
1tsp cornflour
2tbls dry sherry
4oz/100g Chinese
    cabbage, shredded

Trim any fat from the pork and cut meat into thin strips.

Heat the oils and ginger in a wok or frying pan. Add the pork and stir-fry over high heat for 2-3 minutes. Add the water chestnuts and red pepper and stir-fry for a few seconds.

Stir in the prawns. Blend the cornflour with the sherry and pour into the pan. Stir-fry for a few seconds, then stir in the Chinese cabbage and heat through for a few seconds.

Serve at once. **Serves 4**

STIR-FRIED MANGE TOUT

1lb/450g mange tout
5oz/150g baby sweetcorn
    cobs, drained if bottled
salt
2tbls oil
1tbls sesame oil
2oz/50g unsalted cashew
    nuts
4 spring onions, chopped
1tbls soy sauce

Cook the mange tout and sweetcorn, if using fresh, in boiling salted water for 2 minutes, then drain well.

Heat the oils in a wok or frying pan. Add the nuts and stir-fry over high heat until lightly browned. Add the mange tout, sweetcorn, spring onions and soy sauce and stir-fry briefly until heated through.

Serve at once. **Serves 4**

NASI GORENG

1 egg
1 tbls oil
4 tbls peanut or groundnut oil
2 onions, finely chopped
2 garlic cloves, crushed
½ tsp chilli powder
8oz/225g cooked rice
6oz/175g cooked chicken or turkey meat, diced
6oz/175g peeled prawns, defrosted if frozen
2 tbls light soy sauce
1 tsp soft light brown sugar
1 tbls lemon juice
6oz/175g cooked ham, very thinly sliced
black pepper

Beat the egg lightly with 1 tbls water.

Heat 1 tbls oil in a wok or frying pan. Pour in the egg and cook until set underneath. Turn over and cook until set on the other side. Slide the omelette out of the pan and cut into thin strips.

Add the peanut oil to the pan and heat gently. Add the onions, garlic and chilli powder and fry until lightly browned. Add the rice and cook for a few seconds, then stir in the chicken and prawns.

Mix the soy sauce, sugar and lemon juice together, then stir into the rice mixture. Stir in the ham, then season to taste with pepper.

Spoon the mixture into a serving bowl and garnish with the omelette strips. **Serves 4-6**

Note: Nasi Goreng, which means 'fried rice', is extremely popular in Indonesia. It is served alone as a light snack, or as an accompaniment to saté (kebabs).

LAMB SATÉ

Trim any fat and sinew from the lamb, then cut into ½in/1cm slices.

Make the marinade: put 3tbls soy sauce in a shallow dish, add the garlic and black pepper to taste. Stir in the lamb, cover and leave to marinate for 3-4 hours, turning occasionally.

Meanwhile, make the sauce: heat the oil in a saucepan. Add the onion and fry until softened, then stir in the peanut butter, lemon juice, chilli powder, chilli, remaining soy sauce and 3fl oz/85ml water. Cook, stirring, until blended and thick enough to lightly coat the back of the spoon. Pour into a serving dish, dust with paprika and leave to cool.

Drain the meat, reserving the marinade, and thread on to 8-12 wooden skewers. Place on the grill rack and cook under a moderate grill for 10-15 minutes, turning occasionally, until the meat is done to taste. Brush regularly with the marinade to prevent the meat drying out.

Serve the saté at once, garnished with the tomato rose and accompanied with diced cucumber topped with onion rings and the peanut sauce. **Serves 4-6**

1 ½lb/700g lean boneless lamb
1 tomato skin, rolled up to make a rose, to garnish
For the marinade:
4tbls soy sauce
1 garlic clove, crushed
black pepper
For the sauce:
2tbls peanut or groundnut oil
1 small onion, finely chopped
6oz/175g crunchy peanut butter
1tbls lemon juice
½tsp chilli powder
1 small chilli, finely chopped
sweet paprika, for dusting
To serve:
diced peeled cucumber
onion rings

BEEF WITH PEPPERS

8oz/225g beef fillet
3 slices fresh root ginger,
    cut into slivers
1 spring onion, sliced
1 small chilli, seeded and
    sliced
2 small red or green
    peppers, seeded and
    sliced
1 tsp salt
½tsp caster sugar
For the marinade:
3 tbls light soy sauce
2 tsp white wine
2 tsp cornflour
4 tbls oil

Trim any fat from the beef, then cut the meat into thin strips about 1in/2.5cm long.

Make the marinade: mix the soy sauce, wine and cornflour with 1tbls oil and 1tbls water in a shallow dish. Stir in the beef, cover and leave to marinate for 1 hour.

Heat the remaining oil in a wok or frying pan. Add the beef and stir-fry over high heat for 15 seconds. Remove from the pan with a slotted spoon and reserve.

Add the ginger, onion and chilli and stir-fry for a few seconds. Add the peppers and stir-fry for 1-2 minutes.

Return the beef to the pan, add the salt and sugar and stir-fry for 2-3 minutes until the meat is cooked.
Serves 2-3

BEEF IN OYSTER SAUCE

Cut the beef into thin slices.

Make the marinade: mix the soda, cornflour, soy sauce, 1tbls oil, sugar and 3fl oz/85ml water in a shallow dish. Stir in the beef, cover and leave to marinate for 30 minutes.

Prepare the sauce: mix the cornflour, sugar and salt, then stir in the wine, stock and oyster sauce.

Heat remaining oil in a wok or frying pan. Add beef and stir-fry over high heat for 20 seconds. Remove from pan with a slotted spoon and reserve.

Add the garlic, ginger and vegetables and stir-fry until tender but still crisp. Return the beef to the pan. Pour in the sauce and cook, stirring, for a few seconds. Serve at once. **Serves 3-4**

8oz/225g lean beef, trimmed
2 garlic cloves, crushed
2 slices fresh root ginger, cut into slivers
12oz/350g mixed vegetables, sliced
For the marinade:
½tsp bicarbonate of soda
1oz/25g cornflour
1tbls soy sauce
4fl oz/120ml oil
2tsp caster sugar
For the sauce:
½tsp cornflour
1tsp sugar
1tsp salt
2fl oz/50ml white wine
3fl oz/85ml chicken stock
4fl oz/120ml oyster sauce

BARBEQUED SPARERIBS

2½-2¾lb/2.25kg
   American-cut pork
   spareribs
3fl oz/85ml clear honey
spring onion tassels, to
   garnish (optional)
For the marinade:
4oz/100g soft brown sugar
1oz/25g salt
3½fl oz/100ml soy sauce
2½fl oz/65ml white wine
1fl oz/25ml ginger wine
pinch of red food colouring
   powder

Trim any excess fat from the spare ribs. Using a strong, sharp knife, cut between the bones to divide the spareribs into portions of 2-3 chops each.

Make the marinade: mix the sugar, salt, soy sauce, wines and colouring in a shallow dish. Stir in the spareribs, cover and leave to marinate for 1½ hours, turning occasionally.

Drain the spareribs, shaking off any excess marinade and place in a shallow baking tin. Brush with some of the honey, then roast in the oven preheated to 400F/200C/Gas 6 for 25-30 minutes. Turn the spareribs over, brush with the remaining honey and roast for a further 25-30 minutes, until tender.

Serve at once, as a starter, garnished with spring onion tassels if liked. Provide finger bowls and napkins as the spareribs are sticky to eat. **Serves 4-6**

SWEET-SOUR MEAT BALLS

Thinly shred 2oz/50g spring onions and
reserve. Finely chop the rest and place
in a bowl with the mince, cornflour,
soy sauce, wine, salt, ginger and egg.
Mix well, then divide into 16 equal
pieces and form each into a ball.

Prepare the sauce: place the sugar,
cornflour, salt, oil, vinegar and soy
sauce in a saucepan. Mix well, then stir
in the stock. Heat gently, stirring, until
the sauce thickens. Remove from the
heat and reserve.

Pour enough oil into a deep-fat frier
to come one-third of the way up the
sides of the pan. Gently heat the oil to
370F/185C.

Fry the meat balls, in batches, in the
hot oil for about 1 minute or until they
are crisp and golden and float to the
surface. Drain on absorbent paper.

Reheat the oil, then return the meat
balls to the pan and fry for a further 30
seconds. Drain and reserve.

Heat 1tbls oil in a wok or frying pan.
Add the shredded spring onions and
stir-fry for a few seconds. Add the sauce
and bring to the boil. Add the meat
balls and heat through, stirring. Serve
at once, garnished with coriander.

Serves 4

3oz/75g spring onions
8oz/225g minced pork or
   beef
2tbls cornflour
1tbls soy sauce
2tsp white wine
1tsp salt
1/2tsp grated fresh root
   ginger
1 egg, lightly beaten
oil, for frying
coriander sprigs, to
   garnish
For the sauce:
1oz/25g caster sugar
1tbls cornflour
1/2tsp salt
1/2tsp sesame oil
2tsp light malt vinegar
2tsp light soy sauce
1/4 pint/300ml chicken
   stock

SWEET AND SOUR PORK

1lb/450g pork tenderloin,
cut into 1in/2.5cm
cubes
1fl oz/25ml white wine
1tsp sugar
salt and black pepper
3fl oz/85ml light malt
vinegar
2oz/50g caster sugar
4fl oz/120ml tomato
ketchup
8oz/225g can pineapple
pieces, drained, juice
reserved
½ chicken stock cube
3tbls cornflour
1tsp sesame oil
2 egg yolks
oil, for frying
1 onion, finely chopped
2 red or green peppers,
seeded and cut into
cubes

Place pork in a shallow dish and sprinkle with the wine and sugar. Season, cover and reserve.

Meanwhile, mix vinegar, sugar and ketchup together. Make up the pineapple juice to ¼ pint/150ml with hot water, add the stock cube, then stir into the ketchup mixture. Stir in 1tbls cornflour, 1tsp salt and the sesame oil.

In a separate bowl, beat the egg yolks with the remaining cornflour.

Heat oil in a deep-fat frier to 370F/ 185C. Drain pork, dip in the egg yolk mixture and deep fry for 4 minutes or until golden. Drain and reserve.

Heat 2tbls oil in a wok or frying pan. Add onion and stir-fry for 1 minute, then stir in the peppers, ketchup mixture, pork and pineapple pieces. Heat through, stirring. Serve at once.
Serves 6

PORK WITH CASHEWS

8oz/225g lean pork, diced
¼ pint/150ml oil
2oz/50g unsalted cashew
nuts
2 slices fresh root ginger,
shredded
1 carrot, finely sliced
1 spring onion, chopped
1 garlic clove, chopped
For the marinade:
½tsp bicarbonate of soda
2tsp cornflour
1tsp white wine
1fl oz/25ml light soy sauce
salt and black pepper
For the sauce:
½tsp cornflour
1tsp sesame oil
2fl oz/50ml chicken stock
3fl oz/85ml oyster sauce

Make the marinade: blend soda and cornflour with wine and soy sauce in a shallow dish. Season, then stir in the pork and leave to marinate for about 10 minutes.

Meanwhile, prepare the sauce: blend the cornflour with the oil, stock and oyster sauce. Season and reserve.

Heat 2fl oz/50ml oil in a wok or frying pan. Add the nuts and fry until browned, then drain on absorbent paper. Discard the oil.

Heat 2fl oz/50ml oil in the pan. Add the pork and stir-fry over high heat for 1½ minutes, then drain and reserve.

Heat the remaining oil in the pan. Add the ginger, carrot, spring onion and garlic and stir-fry for 1 minute. Return the pork and nuts to the pan. Pour in the sauce, heat through and serve. **Serves 4**

PORK SALAD QUICK FRY

Cut the pork into thin strips and place
in a dish. Sprinkle over the sherry, salt,
cornflour and ginger. Cover and leave
for 30 minutes.

Heat the oil in a wok or frying pan.
Add the pork and stir-fry over high heat
for 2 minutes. Add the leek and stir-fry
for 1 minute. Add the red pepper and
stir-fry for 1 minute, then stir in the
beansprouts. Serve at once. **Serves 4**

8oz/225g pork tenderloin
1tsp dry sherry
½tsp salt
1tsp cornflour
½tsp grated fresh root
  ginger
4tbls oil
1 leek, thinly sliced
1 small red pepper, seeded
  and sliced
4oz/100g beansprouts

ROAST GLAZED DUCK

4lb/1.75kg oven-ready
  duck, defrosted if
  frozen
5tbls soy sauce
4fl oz/120ml dry sherry
2tbls soft brown sugar
½tsp grated fresh root
  ginger
1tsp Chinese Five Spice
  Powder
To garnish:
lettuce leaves
coriander sprigs

Trim any excess fat from the duck, then prick the skin all over with a fork. Place the duck on a rack in a roasting tin and roast in the oven preheated to 350F/180C/Gas 4 for 1½ hours.

Remove the duck and rack from the tin. Pour off all the juices from inside the duck.

Drain off the fat from the tin. Stir the soy sauce, sherry, sugar, ginger and spice powder into the remaining sediment. Bring slowly to the boil, stirring, then remove from the heat.

Return the duck, on the rack, to the tin and baste with the sauce. Roast in the oven for a further 30 minutes, basting regularly with the sauce to give a thick, shiny glaze.

Serve the duck hot or cold, cut into thin slices and garnished with lettuce leaves and coriander. **Serves 4-6**

DUCK CHOW MEIN

5oz/150g egg noodles
salt
4fl oz/120ml oil
4oz/100g duck meat,
  shredded
3oz/75g beansprouts
3oz/75g button
  mushrooms, sliced
3oz/75g spring onions,
  chopped
2tsp soy sauce
½tsp sugar
½tsp sesame oil
1fl oz/25ml white wine
1oz/25g cornflour
7fl oz/200ml chicken
  stock

Cook the noodles in boiling salted water for 4-6 minutes until just tender, then drain and dry on absorbent paper.

Heat 2fl oz/50ml oil in a wok or frying pan. Add the noodles and cook, stirring, until lightly browned, then drain on absorbent paper. Pour off the oil from the pan.

Heat the remaining oil in the pan. Add the duck and stir-fry over high heat for 2-3 minutes. Stir in the beansprouts, mushrooms, spring onions, soy sauce, sugar, sesame oil, wine and 1tsp salt.

Blend the cornflour with the stock and pour into the pan. Stir over low heat until the sauce thickens, then stir in the noodles. Serve at once. **Serves 4**

CHINESE CHICKEN PARCELS

8oz/225g chicken breasts
2tbls soy sauce
1tbls dry sherry
1 garlic clove, crushed
2in/5cm piece fresh root
  ginger, cut into slivers
3-4 spring onions, thinly
  sliced
4oz/100g frozen French
  beans, defrosted and
  finely chopped
oil, for deep frying

Cut the chicken breasts into very thin strips about 1in/2.5cm long.

Mix the soy sauce, sherry and garlic in a bowl, add the chicken and stir well.

Cut 30 x 4in/10cm squares of non-stick baking paper. Brush each square with oil. Divide the chicken between the squares and sprinkle with the ginger, spring onion and beans.

Fold up each square, envelope fashion with 3 corners to the centre, to enclose the chicken filling. Fold each envelope in half to make a rectangle with a pointed flap, then fold the flap over the rectangle to make a neat parcel.

Heat the oil in a deep-fat frier to 370F/185C. Fry the parcels, a few at a time, for 1½-2 minutes each side, turning once.

Drain the parcels thoroughly on absorbent paper. Serve at once.
Serves 4-6

CRISPY CHICKEN SALAD

Heat the oil in a wok or frying pan. Add the celery and stir-fry over high heat for 30 seconds. Add the red pepper and stir-fry for 20 seconds. Add the spinach, then the spring onions and stir-fry for 10 seconds.

Turn off the heat and stir in the chicken, salt, chilli powder and soy sauce.

Serve hot or cold, sprinkled with sesame seeds. **Serves 4**

1 tbls oil
2 celery stalks, thinly sliced
½ red pepper, seeded and sliced
4oz/100g spinach, shredded
2 spring onions, sliced
8oz/225g cooked chicken meat, shredded
½ tsp salt
pinch of chilli powder
1 tbls light soy sauce
2 tsp sesame seeds, toasted

MALAYSIAN FISH

12oz/350g cod fillets,
   skinned and cut into
   cubes
2 tbls lemon juice
2 tbls plain flour
1 tbls curry powder
½ tsp ground ginger
pinch of salt
1 tbls oil
1oz/25g dry roasted
   peanuts
½ pint/300ml fish stock
2 slices fresh or drained
   canned pineapple,
   quartered
onion rings, dipped in
   milk and plain flour and
   fried, to garnish
boiled rice, to serve

Sprinkle the fish with half the lemon juice and set aside for 10 minutes. Meanwhile, mix the flour, curry powder, ginger and salt together in a dish.

Heat the oil in a non-stick frying pan large enough to take the fish in a single layer. Coat the fish in the spiced flour and fry for about 3 minutes, turning once, until the flesh flakes easily when tested with a fork. Remove from the pan and keep hot.

Tip the remaining spiced flour into pan and fry gently for 1 minute. Stir in the nuts, remaining lemon juice and stock. Add fish and pineapple and heat through for 5 minutes.

Transfer to a warmed serving dish and garnish with fried onion rings. Serve at once, with rice. **Serves 3-4**

SINGAPORE SIDE NOODLES

Cook the noodles in boiling salted water for 4-6 minutes, until just tender. Drain well and dry on absorbent paper.

Heat half the oil in a wok or frying pan. Add the noodles and fry briskly until browned. Drain on absorbent paper, arrange on a serving dish and keep hot.

Discard oil in pan. Heat remaining oil, add onion and garlic and fry for 2 minutes, until softened. Add the broccoli, carrot and mushrooms and stir-fry over high heat for 1 minute. Add spring onion, chilli and cabbage and stir-fry for a few seconds.

Blend the cornflour, sugar and salt with the wine. Pour into the pan and cook, stirring, for 20-30 seconds.

Serve at once, on the noodles.

Serves 4-6

4oz/100g egg noodles
4fl oz/120ml oil
1 onion, chopped
2 garlic cloves, chopped
4oz/100g broccoli florets
1 carrot, cut into thin strips
2oz/50g button mushrooms, sliced
1 spring onion, sliced
1 chilli, seeded and thinly sliced
2oz/50g Chinese cabbage, shredded
1 tsp cornflour
pinch of sugar
½ tsp salt
1fl oz/25ml white wine

SWEET AND SOUR CABBAGE

2 fl oz/50ml oil
8oz/225g green cabbage,
　shredded
2 small leeks, thinly sliced
3 dried red chillies, seeded
　and thinly sliced
1 tsp black peppercorns,
　crushed
2 fl oz/50ml light malt
　vinegar
1 tsp sesame oil
1 tsp salt
1oz/25g sugar
1 tsp soy sauce

Heat the oil in a wok or frying pan. Add the cabbage, leeks and chillies and stir-fry over high heat for 2 minutes.

Stir in the peppercorns, vinegar and sesame oil.

Blend the salt, sugar and soy sauce together and stir into the pan. Serve at once. (The vinegar will discolour the cabbage if the dish is left to stand.) **Serves 3-4**

PRAWN CHOP SUEY

1 tbls sunflower oil
1 small onion, chopped
2 carrots, diced
2oz/50g drained canned
　bamboo shoots,
　shredded
1 garlic clove, crushed
1 spring onion, sliced
10oz/275g frozen stir-fry
　vegetables
4oz/100g beansprouts
7oz/200g can peeled
　prawns, drained
½tsp cornflour
1 tsp ginger wine
1 tbls light soy sauce
1 tbls sherry

Heat the oil in a wok or frying pan. Add the onion and carrots and stir-fry over high heat for 1 minute. Add the bamboo shoots, garlic, spring onion and frozen vegetables and stir-fry for 2 minutes. Add the beansprouts and prawns and stir-fry for 1 minute.

Blend the cornflour with the wine, soy sauce and sherry. Add to the pan and heat through, stirring, for 1 minute. Serve at once. **Serves 4-6**

COCONUT PUDDINGS

7oz/200g creamed
    coconut
¾ pint/450ml warm milk
2 sachets powdered
    gelatine
3oz/75g caster sugar
red and green glacé
    cherries, to decorate

Place the coconut in a mixing bowl and
break it up with a fork. Gradually stir in
the milk.

Sprinkle the gelatine over 8tbls water
in a heatproof bowl and leave to soak
for 1-2 minutes. Stand the bowl in a
pan of hot water and leave until the
gelatine has melted, stirring
occasionally. Add the sugar and stir
until dissolved.

Stir the dissolved gelatine into the
coconut milk. Leave until thickened,
but not set.

Rinse out 6 individual jelly moulds
with cold water. Pour the coconut jelly
into the moulds, then cover and chill
for 2-3 hours, until set.

To serve: loosen the edges of 1
pudding from the sides of the mould.
Dip the mould in hot water for 1-2
seconds, then invert a serving plate on
top. Hold plate and mould firmly and
invert, giving a sharp shake halfway
round. Lift off mould. Turn out
remaining puddings in the same way.
Decorate with cherries. **Serves 6**

FRUIT FRITTERS

Cut the fruit into even-sized pieces.

Sift the flour and cornflour into a bowl. Make a well in the centre. Add the egg yolks and ¼ pint/150ml water and beat well to make a smooth batter.

Make the caramel: put the sugar into a heavy-based saucepan with 4fl oz/120ml water and stir over low heat until dissolved. Bring to the boil and boil briskly, without stirring, until the syrup turns a light caramel colour. Remove pan from the heat and plunge the base into warm water.

Heat the oil in a deep-fat frier to 370F/185C.

Whisk the egg whites until stiff, then fold into the batter.

Dip the fruit, a few pieces at a time, in the batter and fry in the hot oil for about 5 minutes, until crisp and golden. Drain on absorbent paper and keep hot. Coat and fry the remaining fruit in the same way.

Place the fritters on an oiled plate. Pour the caramel over the fritters, turning pieces with a fork so they are evenly coated. Sprinkle with the sesame seeds and serve at once.

Serves 4

2 bananas
2 dessert apples,
    quartered and cored
oil, for deep frying
2tbls sesame seeds,
    toasted
For the batter:
3oz/75g plain flour
1oz/25g cornflour
2 eggs, separated
For the caramel:
4oz/100g caster sugar

MEXICO AND THE CARIBBEAN

GUACAMOLE

2 small avocados
1 tbls lemon juice
1 small onion, finely
  chopped
1 green chilli, seeded and
  finely chopped
1 tbls finely chopped
  coriander leaves
1 tomato, finely chopped
salt and black pepper
tortilla or corn chips, to
  serve

Halve and stone the avocados. Scoop out the flesh into a bowl, add the lemon juice and mash well. Stir in the onion, chilli, coriander and tomato and season to taste.

Spoon into a serving dish. Serve with tortilla or corn chips. **Serves 4**

CHICKEN AND CHILLI SALAD

1 tbls peanut or groundnut
  oil
2 tsp lemon juice
salt and black pepper
2 spring onions, chopped
2 large green tomatoes,
  finely chopped
12 oz/350g cooked chicken
  meat, diced
3 oz/75g salted peanuts
3 slices fresh or drained
  canned pineapple,
  chopped
1 red chilli, seeded and
  sliced
2-3 oz/50-75g Chinese
  cabbage, shredded

Place the oil and lemon juice in a bowl, season and whisk well with a fork. Stir in the spring onions and tomatoes.

Place the chicken, peanuts, pineapple and chilli in a separate bowl. Stir in two-thirds of the tomato mixture, mixing well.

Arrange the cabbage over the base of a serving dish. Spoon the chicken salad in the centre and top with the remaining tomato mixture. **Serves 4-6**

MEXICAN CHICKEN

4-6 chicken joints
2tbls lemon juice
For the sauce:
4oz/100g creamed
    coconut
2tbls oil
1 large onion, chopped
1 garlic clove, chopped
4oz/100g crunchy peanut
    butter
2tbls drinking chocolate
    powder
salt and black pepper
lime slices, halved, to
    garnish

Place the chicken joints in a single layer in a dish. Prick the skin all over with a fork, then sprinkle with the lemon juice. Cover and leave for 30 minutes.

Place the chicken on a grill rack and cook under a medium grill for 25-30 minutes until tender, turning once.

About 10 minutes before the chicken is ready, make the sauce. Break up the coconut with a fork. Slowly add ½ pint/300ml warm water, stirring to dissolve the coconut.

Heat the oil in a saucepan. Add the onion and garlic and fry gently until lightly browned. Stir in the coconut liquid and cook for 2-3 minutes. Stir in the peanut butter and drinking chocolate and season. Cook gently for 2 minutes to heat through.

Place the grilled chicken joints on a serving dish and spoon the sauce on top. Garnish with slices of lime and serve at once. **Serves 4-6**

COURGETTE CASSEROLE

Heat the oil in a flameproof casserole dish. Add the onion and fry until softened. Add the garlic and red pepper and cook, stirring, for 5 minutes.

Stir in the courgettes, sweetcorn and kidney beans and season.

Cover tightly and bake in the oven preheated to 350F/180C/Gas 4 for 20-25 minutes, until the courgettes are tender. Check the seasoning and serve.

Serves 4-6

2 tbls peanut or groundnut oil
1 onion, chopped
2 garlic cloves, crushed
1 red pepper, seeded and sliced
1lb/450g courgettes, thinly sliced
11oz/300g can sweetcorn
15oz/425g can red kidney beans, drained and rinsed
salt and black pepper

RUM ROAST PORK

3¼-4lb/1.5-1.75kg loin
of pork
½tsp ground ginger
¼tsp ground cloves
2 garlic cloves, crushed
salt and black pepper
6fl oz/175ml dark rum
½-¾ pint/300-450ml
chicken stock
3oz/75g soft dark brown
sugar
juice of 2 oranges
1½tsp arrowroot
To garnish:
orange slices
coriander sprigs

Ask the butcher to chine the pork and score the fat.

Weigh the joint and calculate the exact cooking time: allow 30 minutes per 1lb/450g plus an extra 30 minutes.

Mix the spices and garlic and season generously. Rub the mixture into the scored skin, making sure it penetrates down to the fat. Place the pork on a rack in a roasting tin. Pour half the rum and ¼ pint/150ml chicken stock into the tin. Roast in the oven preheated to 350F/180C/Gas 4 for about 1 hour, or half the calculated cooking time.

Mix the sugar, orange juice and remaining rum. Spoon some of the mixture over the pork. Roast the joint for a further 1 hour, or the remaining calculated cooking time. Spoon more orange rum over the joint several times during roasting until it is used up and add another ¼ pint/150ml stock to the tin if necessary.

Transfer the pork to a serving dish.

Drain excess fat from the juices in the tin. Measure the tin juices and make up to ¾ pint/450ml with some of the remaining stock if necessary. Place the arrowroot in a saucepan and slowly blend in the measured juices. Bring to the boil and simmer, stirring, until the sauce thickens and clears.

Garnish the pork. Serve with the sauce. **Serves 4-6**

OKRA AND PRAWN SOUP

2tbls oil
4oz/100g okra, sliced
1¾ pints/1 litre fish stock
made with 2 cubes
8oz/225g peeled prawns,
defrosted if frozen
¼tsp chilli powder
1 tomato, chopped

Heat the oil in a saucepan. Add the okra and fry briskly, turning frequently, for about 1 minute until softened.

Pour in the stock. Add the prawns, chilli powder and tomato. Stir well, then cook gently for 10-15 minutes.

Serve at once. **Serves 4**

CARIBBEAN FISH SOUP

Skin the fillets and remove any bones, then cut into 1in/2.5cm cubes.

Heat the oil in a saucepan. Add the onion and garlic and cook until light golden. Add the rice and fish and cook for 5 minutes, stirring gently.

Add the vegetables and stock. Bring to the boil, then lower the heat and cook gently for 10-15 minutes. Add the crabmeat and cook gently for a further 10 minutes. Season to taste.

Serve at once, sprinkled with coriander. **Serves 4**

1lb/450g white fish fillets
3tbls oil
1 onion, chopped
1 garlic clove, crushed
2oz/50g long grain rice
1 tomato, chopped
1 potato, chopped
4oz/100g cabbage, shredded
1 small green pepper, sliced
1¾ pints/1 litre fish stock
4oz/100g canned crabmeat
salt and black pepper
chopped coriander leaves

VENEZUELAN STEWED BEEF

1/1 ¼lb/500g flank of beef
1 turnip, chopped
1 carrot, chopped
1 leek, sliced
2 tbls peanut or groundnut oil
1 large onion, chopped
1 garlic clove, crushed
1 small green pepper, seeded and sliced
1 red chilli, seeded and sliced
2 tomatoes, chopped
pinch of ground cinnamon
pinch of ground cloves
To serve:
boiled rice
15oz/425g can red kidney beans, heated and drained

Cut the meat into thin slices and place in a heavy-based saucepan with the turnip, carrot and leek. Pour in ½ pint/300ml water and cook gently for about 1½ hours until the meat is tender.

Remove the meat with a slotted spoon and reserve. Strain the stock, discarding the vegetables.

Heat the oil in the rinsed out saucepan. Add the onion and garlic, cover and cook gently for about 5 minutes until softened. Stir in the green pepper, chilli, tomatoes and spices. Add the meat and ½ pint/300ml strained stock. Season, then cook gently for 10-15 minutes until the green pepper is tender and the stew is piping hot.

Serve the stew with rice and kidney beans. **Serves 4-6**

CHILLI CON CARNE

Heat the oil in a large heavy-based saucepan. Add the beef and fry briskly until browned on all sides. Transfer to a plate with a slotted spoon.

Add the onion and garlic to the pan and fry gently until lightly browned. Stir in the chilli powder and cook for 3-5 seconds. Stir in the tomato purée, oregano, cumin, tomatoes and stock.

Return the meat to the pan and season with salt. Cover and cook gently for 1½ hours, or until the meat is tender.

Serve hot, sprinkled with chilli rings.

Serves 4-6

3 tbls oil
1¼lb/500g chuck steak, cut into small cubes
1 large onion, chopped
1 garlic clove, chopped
2 tsp chilli powder
2 tbls tomato purée
1 tsp dried oregano
½ tsp ground cumin
8oz/225g can tomatoes
½ pint/300ml beef stock
salt
1 red chilli, seeded and sliced into thin rings, to garnish

TOSTADAS WITH CHORIZOS

6 tostada shells
For the filling:
1lb/450g can refried beans
1-2oz/25-50g Chinese
  cabbage, shredded
2 tomatoes, thinly sliced
3 chorizos, chopped
guacamole, made with 2
  avocados (see p34)
1 red onion, thinly sliced
  and separated into rings

Place the tostada shells on a baking sheet and heat in the oven preheated to 350F/180C/Gas 4 for 5-10 minutes.

Meanwhile, heat the beans in a saucepan.

Remove the tostada shells from the oven and divide the beans between them. Sprinkle a little sliced cabbage over each portion of beans and top with tomato slices, chopped sausage and guacamole.

Garnish with onion rings and serve. **Serves 6**

SALAD STUFFED TACOS

6 taco shells
For the filling:
7oz/200g can beef taco
  filling
1-2oz/25-50g Chinese
  cabbage, shredded
2oz/50g slice of ham, cut
  into thin strips
2oz/50g Edam cheese, cut
  into thin strips
3-4 radishes, thinly sliced
3-4tsp hot tomato and
  chilli sauce
To serve (optional):
pickled green chillies
extra hot tomato and chilli
  sauce

Place the taco shells on a baking sheet and bake in the oven preheated to 350F/180C/Gas 4, for 5-10 minutes.

Remove the shells from the oven and divide the beef filling between them. Sprinkle a little of the sliced cabbage over each filling and top with the ham, cheese and radishes. Drizzle over the tomato and chilli sauce.

Serve at once, with the remaining cabbage, pickled green chillies and extra sauce if liked. **Serves 6**

PINEAPPLE DELIGHT

3oz/75g long strand or
desiccated coconut
1 pineapple
6oz/175g demerara sugar
2oz/50g unsalted butter
2oz/50g shelled Brazil
nuts, finely chopped

Place the coconut in a bowl, cover with hot water and leave to soften for about 10 minutes.

Meanwhile, cut the top off the pineapple with a serrated knife. Reserve some of the leaves. Cut the skin off the pineapple and remove any spiky brown bits from the flesh. Chop the pineapple flesh, discarding any tough woody core.

Place the chopped pineapple and sugar in a large non-stick frying pan and stir over low heat until the sugar has melted. Add the butter.

Drain the coconut and add to the pan. Cook, stirring occasionally, for about 30 minutes until the juice from the pineapple has evaporated. Remove from the heat and stir in the nuts.

Pile the mixture on to a serving dish and decorate with the reserved leaves. Serve hot or cold. **Serves 4-6**

BRAZILIAN BANANAS

4 bananas, unpeeled
2 small mangoes,
unpeeled
2tbls lemon juice
lime slices, halved
To serve (optional):
¼ pint/150ml double
cream, lightly whipped
2tbls molasses or rich dark
brown sugar

Place the bananas on a baking sheet. Bake in the oven preheated to 400F/200C/Gas 6 for 10 minutes or until the skins have turned black.

Meanwhile, cut the mangoes into slices, discarding the large stone. Cut off the peel, if preferred.

Remove the bananas from the oven. Cut a sliver of skin from the base of each banana so that they will sit upright. Make 2 parallel cuts along the top of each banana, then peel away the centre section of skin. Sprinkle the exposed banana flesh with lemon juice.

Place the bananas on serving dishes and top with mango and lime slices.

Place the cream in a bowl, sprinkle with sugar and serve with the bananas, if liked. **Serves 4**

SPICED COFFEE

Place the sugar in a small, heavy-based saucepan. Pour in ¼pint/150ml water. Add the cinnamon and nutmeg and bring slowly to the boil, stirring. Simmer for 4 minutes, then remove from the heat.

Strain the spiced syrup into the hot coffee. Pour the spiced coffe into a coffee pot and serve at once; or, leave the coffee to cool, then chill for 2 hours before serving.

Serve with cream or milk, if liked.

Serves 4-6

4tbls molasses or rich dark
  brown sugar
1 cinnamon stick
large pinch of freshly
  grated nutmeg
1 pint/600ml hot black
  coffee
cream or milk, to serve
  (optional)

INDIA

TANDOORI CHICKEN

2½lb/2.25kg chicken
  pieces, skinned
1 tbls lemon juice
½ tsp salt
For the marinade:
½ pint/300ml natural
  yoghurt
1 small onion
2 thin slices fresh root
  ginger
½ tsp red food colouring
  powder
½ tsp chilli powder
For the garnish:
lettuce leaves
lime wedges

Make small slits in the chicken meat with a sharp knife. Place the chicken pieces in a dish large enough to hold them in a single layer and sprinkle evenly with the lemon juice and salt.

Place the yoghurt, onion, ginger, colouring powder and chilli powder in a blender or food processor and blend until smooth. Pour the marinade over the chicken. Cover the dish with cling film and refrigerate for 8 hours, or overnight, turning the pieces occasionally.

Place the chicken on a greased baking tray and spoon over any marinade remaining in the dish. Cook in the oven preheated to 450F/230C/ Gas 8 for 15-20 minutes, until the chicken is tender and the juices run clear when tested with a fork.

Transfer the chicken to a warmed serving dish, garnish and serve.
Serves 4

SPICED BROCCOLI

1lb/450g broccoli spears
salt
2oz/50g unsalted butter
1 tsp cumin seeds
2 tbls cornflour
1 tsp grated fresh root
  ginger
2 thin slices fresh root
  ginger, cut into slivers,
  to garnish

Cook the broccoli in boiling salted water until tender, then drain well and mash.

Heat the butter in a frying pan until melted and hot. Add the cumin seeds and cook for 2 seconds until lightly browned. Stir in the cornflour, grated ginger and mashed broccoli. Season to taste with salt.

Cook, stirring, until heated through, then spoon into a warmed serving dish. Sprinkled with the slivered ginger and serve at once. **Serves 4**

CHILLI CHICKEN

4 chicken joints
4 spring onions
2 green chillies
2 thin slices fresh root
    ginger
2 garlic cloves, chopped
1/2 pint/300ml soured
    cream
thin rings of red and green
    chilli, to garnish

Select a flameproof casserole or deep frying pan, with a lid, large enough to hold the chicken joints in a single layer. Place the chicken in the casserole with the spring onions, chillies, ginger and garlic. Pour in 1/2 pint/300ml water and bring slowly to the boil. Cover and simmer very gently for about 30 minutes, until the chicken is tender.

Remove the chicken from the casserole and set aside to cool.

Meanwhile, bring the cooking liquid in the casserole to the boil and boil until reduced to about 3fl oz/85ml. Remove from the heat. Discard the chillies, ginger and garlic.

Remove chicken meat from the bones and cut it into pieces. Add the chicken meat to the reduced stock, then stir in the soured cream. Return to low heat and heat through gently, without boiling.

Garnish with chilli rings and serve.
Serves 4-6

SPICED OKRA

5 tbls oil
1 lb/450g okra, cut into
    1 in/2.5cm lengths
1 onion, chopped
2 garlic cloves, crushed
1 tsp grated fresh root
    ginger
1 tsp tamarind extract
1 tsp salt
1 tbls chopped coriander
    leaves, to garnish

Heat the oil in a non-stick frying pan. Add the okra and fry briskly for 2-3 minutes, stirring constantly. Remove the okra from the pan with a slotted spoon and reserve.

Add the onion to the pan and fry gently until softened. Add the garlic and ginger and fry for 1 minute.

Dissolve the tamarind in 1/4 pint/150ml hot water and pour into the pan. Add the salt and stir well to mix. Return the okra to the pan, cover and cook gently for about 15 minutes, until tender.

Spoon the spiced okra into a warmed serving dish, sprinkle with coriander and serve. **Serves 4**

CURRIED LAMB

5tbls oil
2 onions, sliced
1½lb/700g top leg of
　lamb, boned and cut
　into 1inch/2.5cm cubes
2 garlic cloves, crushed
1tsp grated fresh root
　ginger
1tsp ground cumin
1tsp ground coriander
¼tsp turmeric
¼tsp cayenne pepper
2tbls natural yoghurt
2oz/50g seedless raisins
1tsp salt
¼ pint/150ml double
　cream
1tsp garam masala
chopped coriander leaves,
　to garnish

Heat 4tbls oil in a large flameproof casserole. Add the onions and fry until golden. Transfer half the onions to a piece of absorbent paper. Fry the remaining onions until deep brown, then transfer to a separate piece of absorbent paper and reserve for garnish.

Add the remaining oil to the pan. Add the meat and fry briskly until lightly browned on all sides. Using a slotted spoon, transfer the meat to a plate.

Add the garlic, ginger, cumin, coriander, turmeric, cayenne and the batch of golden onions to the pan. Add the yoghurt, stirring until blended, then stir in ¾ pint/450ml water. Return the meat to the pan, cover and cook gently for about 1 hour, until the meat is tender.

Stir in the raisins, salt, cream and garam masala. Garnish with chopped coriander and the reserved fried onions and serve. **Serves 4-6**

VEGETABLE PILAU

Cook rice in boiling salted water for
4 minutes, until tender, then drain.

Pour 3tbls boiling water over the
saffron and set aside.

Fry cumin seeds and vegetables in the
oil for 2 minutes. Transfer vegetables to
a plate.

Add butter to pan. Add onion and fry
gently for 3 minutes, then stir in the
turmeric, coriander, rice, vegetables
and salt to taste. Add saffron liquid.
Cover pan with foil and the lid and
leave over low heat for 2 minutes.
Uncover, stir well and serve.
Serves 4-6

*6oz/175g basmati rice,
  cleaned (see p4)*
salt
*¼tsp saffron strands,
  ground (see p5)*
1tsp cumin seeds
*¾-1lb/350-450g mixed
  broccoli florets, diced
  carrots, peas and sliced
  French beans*
6tbls oil
1oz/25g butter
4oz/100g onion, chopped
½tsp turmeric
½tsp ground coriander

PINEAPPLE PICKLE

Grind the chilli powder, mustard seeds,
garlic and ginger together.

Heat the oil in a saucepan. Add the
chilli and cook for 1-2 seconds. Stir in
the ground spices, sugar, salt and
vinegar. Bring to the boil and cook for 2
minutes. Stir in the pineapple and cook
for 2 minutes more. Cool. Keep in an
airtight jar for up to 1 week. **Makes
about 1 pint/600ml**

1tsp chilli powder
1tbls mustard seeds
2 garlic cloves
*1tsp grated fresh root
  ginger*
3fl oz/85ml oil
1 dried red chilli
2tbls soft brown sugar
½tsp salt
*7fl oz/200ml light malt
  vinegar*
*1 pineapple, peeled and
  finely chopped*

SAMOSAS

8oz/225g plain flour
salt
4tbls oil
oil, for deep frying
coriander sprigs, to
garnish
For the filling:
2tbls oil
2oz/50g onion, finely
chopped
2 garlic cloves, crushed
1tsp grated fresh root
ginger
1 green chilli, seeded and
chopped
½tsp ground coriander
½tsp ground cumin
1lb/450g minced beef or
lamb
4oz/100g potato, diced
4oz/100g peas
1tbls chopped mint
2tsp lemon juice
1½tsp garam masala

Sift flour and ½tsp salt into a bowl.
Work in 4tbls oil with your fingertips.
Stir in 5tbls tepid water and mix to a
dough. Knead for 10 minutes. Reserve
in an oiled polythene bag.

Make the filling: heat the oil in a
saucepan. Add the onion, garlic and
ginger and fry gently until softened.
Stir in the chilli, coriander, cumin and
mince. Pour in ¼ pint/150ml water and
cook for 15 minutes. Add potatoes and
peas and cook for a further 10 minutes.
Stir in mint, 1tsp salt, lemon juice and
garam masala. Leave until cold.

Divide the dough into 8 equal balls.
Return 7 balls to the bag. Roll out the
remaining ball to a 7in/18cm round and
cut in half. Dampen edges of 1 semi-
circle with water, then shape into a
cone. Press the joins to seal. Spoon in a
little filling, then crimp top edges
together. Shape and fill the other semi-
circle in the same way. Make 14 more
samosas from the remaining dough.

Heat oil in a deep-fat frier to 370F/
185C. Fry the samosas, in batches,
until golden, turning once. Drain and
serve. **Makes 16**

KOFTAS

Mix the mince with 2tbls yoghurt, coriander, garam masala and ½tsp salt. Divide into 40 small balls.

Make the sauce: heat the oil in a large saucepan. Add the onion and fry until softened. Stir in the ginger, garlic, cardamom and cloves and cook briskly for 2 minutes. Stir in the cinnamon, cumin and 1tsp salt. Add the tomatoes and heat through, then stir in remaining yoghurt.

Add the meat balls to the sauce, cover and simmer gently for about 25 minutes, until cooked.

Transfer the meat balls to a serving dish and keep hot. Boil the sauce until reduced and thickened, then spoon over meat balls. Garnish with mooli slices. **Serves 4**

1lb/450g minced beef or lamb
4tbls natural yoghurt
2tbls chopped coriander leaves
1tsp garam masala
salt
mooli slices, to garnish
For the sauce:
4tbls oil
1 onion, chopped
½tsp grated fresh root ginger
2 garlic cloves, crushed
8 cardamom pods
6 cloves
½tsp ground cinnamon
1tsp ground cumin
14oz/400g can chopped tomatoes

SPICED BEEF

1¼lb/500g lean beef, cut
  into thin strips
2tbls fresh lime juice
12oz/350g onions
4fl oz/120ml oil
8 cloves
10 cardamom pods
2 fresh chillies
1 dried red chilli
2 tomatoes, chopped
1 tsp tamarind extract,
  dissolved in ¼ pint/
  150ml hot water
1 tsp sugar
1 tsp garam masala
coriander leaves, to
  garnish

Sprinkle the beef with the lime juice.

Thinly slice half the onions into rings; chop the rest. Heat the oil in a large saucepan. Add onion rings and fry until well browned, then drain and reserve.

Fry the beef until browned on all sides, then transfer to a plate. Add the chopped onions and fry until softened. Add the cloves, cardamom and chillies and fry for 2 seconds. Stir in the tomatoes and tamarind liquid.

Return the beef to the pan. Add the sugar and garam masala. Cook gently, stirring occasionally, for ¾-1 hour, until the beef is tender. Add a little water during cooking, if necessary, to prevent drying out. Serve garnished with fried onion rings and coriander.
Serves 4

SPECKLED RICE

Cook the rice in boiling salted water for 4 minutes or until just tender. Drain well, cover and keep warm.

Heat the oil and butter in a saucepan until the butter has melted. Add the spring onions and chilli and fry for 2 minutes. Stir in the ground coriander and cook, stirring, for 2 seconds.

Remove the pan from the heat. Add the rice, mounding it in the centre of the pan. Add 1 tsp salt, the chopped mint and coriander and 2 tbls water. Cover the pan with a double layer of foil and the lid. Return the pan to very low heat for 5 minutes.

Uncover and stir well. Spoon into a serving dish and garnish with mint.

Serves 4-6

6oz/175g basmati rice,
   cleaned (see p4)
salt
1 tbls oil
1oz/25g unsalted butter
4 spring onions, sliced
1 green chilli
2 tsp ground coriander
3 tbls chopped mint
4 tbls chopped coriander
   leaves
mint sprig, to garnish

CUCUMBER RELISH

¾ cucumber, coarsely
    grated
1 tsp salt
½ tsp garam masala
3 tbls chopped coriander
    leaves
½ pint/300ml natural
    yoghurt
sweet paprika, for dusting

Sprinkle the cucumber with the salt
and leave to stand for 30 minutes.

Stir the garam masala and coriander
into the yoghurt.

Drain the cucumber, then stir into
the yoghurt. Turn the relish into a
serving dish and dust with paprika.
Serves 4-6

ROGAN JOSH

5 tbls oil
1½lb/700g chuck steak,
    trimmed and cut into
    1in/2.5cm cubes
1in/2.5cm piece
    cinnamon stick
1 tsp coriander seeds
6 cloves
2 onions, chopped
1 tsp grated fresh root
    ginger
½ tsp ground coriander
1 tsp ground cumin
1 tbls sweet paprika
¼ tsp cayenne pepper
½ tsp chilli powder
1 tsp salt
14oz/400g can peeled
    tomatoes
coriander sprigs, to
    garnish
cooked poppadums, to
    serve

Heat 4tbls oil in a saucepan. Add the
meat and fry briskly until browned on
all sides, then transfer to a plate.

Add the remaining oil to the pan.
Add the cinnamon, coriander seeds and
cloves and cook for 2 seconds. Stir in
the onions and fry gently until
softened. Stir in the ginger, ground
coriander, cumin, paprika, cayenne
and chilli powder and cook for 2
seconds.

Return the meat to the pan, then stir
in the salt. Add the tomatoes and bring
to the boil. Lower the heat, cover and
cook for about 2 hours, until the meat is
tender.

Spoon the meat and sauce on to
heated serving plates. Garnish with
coriander and serve at once, with
poppadums. **Serves 4-6**

KABAB

1 lb/450g minced beef or
  lamb
2 small onions, finely
  chopped
2 garlic cloves, crushed
1 chilli, seeded and
  chopped
2 tbls chopped coriander
  leaves
1 tsp grated fresh root
  ginger
1 tsp ground cumin
1 tsp ground coriander
½ tsp ground cloves
¼ tsp ground nutmeg
¼ tsp ground cinnamon
salt and black pepper
1 egg, beaten
To garnish:
1 red onion, sliced into
  rings
coriander sprigs
lemon wedges

Place the mince in a mixing bowl. Add the chopped onion, garlic, chilli, chopped coriander, ginger and ground spices. Season well, then add the egg and mix thoroughly until evenly blended.

Divide the mixture into 8 equal pieces, shape each into a pattie and place on a grill rack. Cook the patties under a moderate grill for 10-15 minutes, turning once, until lightly browned.

Transfer the patties to a warmed serving dish. Garnish with onion rings, coriander sprigs and lemon wedges and serve at once. **Serves 4**

TOMATO RELISH

Mix the tomatoes with the onion, garam masala, lemon juice and coriander.

Spoon the mixture into a serving dish. Serve at room temperature, or cover and chill if preferred. **Serves 4**

3 tomatoes, chopped
2 tbls chopped onion
¼ tsp garam masala
1 tbls lemon juice
2 tbls chopped coriander
  leaves

SWEET-SOUR CHICK-PEAS

Heat the oil in a saucepan. Add the onion and fry for 5 minutes. Stir in the chilli and ginger and cook for 1 minute. Stir in the ground coriander, cumin and garam masala.

Dissolve the tamarind in ¼ pint/150ml hot water and add to the pan. Stir in the chick-peas and salt and mix well. Cook gently, stirring occasionally, for 10-15 minutes to allow the flavours to develop and mingle.

Transfer the mixture to a serving dish and sprinkle with coriander. Serve hot or cold. **Serves 4-6**

3 tbls oil
1 onion, chopped
1 green chilli, seeded and
  chopped
1 tsp grated fresh root
  ginger
2 tsp ground coriander
2 tsp ground cumin
1 tsp garam masala
1 tsp tamarind extract
15oz/425g can chick-
  peas, drained and
  rinsed
1 tsp salt
chopped coriander leaves,
  to garnish

MARINATED LEG OF LAMB

4lb/1.75kg leg of lamb,
   aitch bone removed
½oz/15g blanched
   almonds, cut into slivers
2tbls sultanas, cut in half
2 chilli tassels (see p4), to
   garnish
For the marinade:
2 onions, coarsely chopped
6 garlic cloves
2tbls ground coriander
1tbls ground cumin
1tsp salt
2 green chillies, seeded
½ pint/300ml natural
   yoghurt

Using a sharp knife, trim all the skin and fat from the lamb, then make a few 3in/8cm slits in the meat. Transfer the lamb to a large dish.

To make the marinade, place the onions, garlic, ground spices, salt, chillies and a little yoghurt in a blender or food processor and blend until fairly smooth. Stir in the remaining yoghurt.

Pour the marinade over the lamb. Cover and refrigerate for 24 hours, turning occasionally and rubbing the marinade into the slits.

Transfer the lamb to a large piece of foil in a roasting tin. Spoon over the remaining marinade. Wrap the meat loosely in the foil. Bake in the oven preheated to 400F/200C/Gas 6 for 2 hours. Open the foil and sprinkle the almonds and sultanas over the lamb. Bake the lamb, uncovered, for a further 10 minutes.

Remove the tin from the oven. Close the foil over the lamb and leave to stand for 10 minutes to make carving easier.

Serve garnished with chilli tassels.
Serves 6-8

CHANA DAL WITH SPINACH

Place the chana dal in a large saucepan with the sliced ginger and 2 pints/1.2 litres water. Bring to the boil, then cover and simmer for 20-30 minutes, or until tender. Drain well and discard the ginger.

Heat the oil and butter in a non-stick saucepan. Add the grated ginger and garlic and cook gently, stirring, for 1 minute. Stir in the cumin, salt and spinach and cook briskly for 2 minutes.

Add the chana dal and mix well. Cook gently, stirring frequently, for 5 minutes to heat through.

Serve at once. **Serves 4-6**

8oz/225g chana dal or yellow split peas, rinsed
2 thin slices fresh root ginger
2tbls oil
1oz/25g unsalted butter
1tsp grated fresh root ginger
2 garlic cloves, crushed
1tbls ground cumin
1tsp salt
8oz/225g spinach, shredded

INDIAN-STYLE FISH

12oz/350g haddock fillets
(tail pieces if possible)
1 tsp turmeric
1 tsp grated fresh root
ginger
½tsp chilli powder
salt and black pepper
2 tbls light malt vinegar
1 garlic clove, crushed
oil, for deep frying
lime wedges, to garnish

Skin the fillets and cut the flesh into 1in/2.5cm wide strips.

Place the turmeric, grated ginger and chilli powder in a shallow dish. Add 1tsp salt, 1tsp pepper, the vinegar and garlic and mix together.

Heat the oil in a deep-fat frier to 370F/185C.

Coat half the fish in the spice mixture, then fry in the hot oil for about 5 minutes, until crisp and golden. Drain on absorbent paper. Keep warm while you coat and fry the remaining fish in the same way.

Garnish the fish with lime wedges and serve at once. **Serves 3-4**

MANGO CHUTNEY

2 mangoes
3 garlic cloves
2 tsp chilli powder
1 tsp ground ginger
½tsp mustard seeds
pinch of turmeric
2 fl oz/50ml oil
¼ pint/150ml light malt
vinegar
2 tbls soft light brown
sugar

Peel the mangoes and cut the flesh away from the large stone. Chop the mango flesh and reserve.

Grind the garlic with the chilli powder, ginger, mustard seeds and turmeric in an electric mill or pound finely using a mortar and pestle.

Heat the oil in saucepan. Add the ground spices and fry for 2 seconds. Stir in the vinegar and sugar. Stir over low heat until the sugar has dissolved, then bring to the boil and simmer for 2 minutes.

Add the chopped mangoes. Bring back to the boil and cook gently for 5 minutes, taking care the fruit does not disintegrate.

Leave to cool, then pour into an airtight container. Cover tightly and store for at least 2 days before serving. Use within 1 week. **Makes about ½ pint/300ml**

LENTILS WITH POTATOES

Place the lentils in a saucepan with the onion, garlic and 2 pints/1.2 litres water. Bring to the boil, then cover and simmer gently for about 15 minutes.

Add the potato and turmeric and cook for a further 10 minutes, or until the lentils and potato are tender.

Stir in the salt, butter and soured cream. Serve at once. **Serves 4-6**

8oz/225g red lentils, rinsed
1 onion, chopped
1 garlic clove
1 waxy potato, diced
½tsp turmeric
1tsp salt
½oz/15g butter
2tbls soured cream

AUBERGINES IN HOT SAUCE

4fl oz/120ml oil, plus
  extra if necessary
2 aubergines, thickly
  sliced and cut into
  wedges
2 spring onions, sliced
2 garlic cloves, crushed
½tsp grated fresh root
  ginger
8fl oz/250ml tomato
  ketchup
1tbls hot chilli and tomato
  sauce
½tsp salt
chopped coriander leaves,
  to garnish

Heat the oil in a large non-stick frying pan. Fry the aubergines, in batches, until browned on each side. Use a slotted spoon to remove each batch from the pan and add a little more oil if necessary. Add the spring onions, garlic and ginger to the pan and cook, stirring, for 2 minutes. Stir in ketchup, chilli sauce, salt and ¼ pint/150ml water.

Return the aubergines to the pan and cook gently for 10-15 minutes, stirring occasionally, until tender.

Turn into a warmed serving dish, sprinkle with coriander and serve.
Serves 4-6

POORIS

8oz/225g wholemeal flour
½tsp salt
2tbls oil
oil, for deep frying
mint sprigs, to garnish

Sift the flour and salt into a mixing bowl. Discard the residue of bran in the sieve. Add the oil and work it in with the fingertips of one hand. Pour in ¼ pint/150ml warm water and mix to a dough.

Turn out the dough on to a clean surface and knead until smooth. Shape into a ball, place in an oiled polythene bag and leave for 30 minutes.

Knead the dough briefly, then divide into 12 equal pieces. Return 11 pieces to the bag. Shape the remaining piece into a ball and roll out thinly to a 5½in/14cm round. Place on a lightly oiled tray and cover with cling film. Shape the remaining dough in the same way.

Heat the oil in a deep-fat frier to 370F/185C. Fry the pooris individually for about 10 seconds, carefully turning them over with a fish slice as they rise and puff on the surface. Drain on absorbent paper and keep hot while you fry each remaining pooris.

Serve at once, garnished with mint.
Makes 12

CAULIFLOWER CURRY

1 cauliflower
5 tbls oil
1 onion, chopped
2 garlic cloves, crushed
½ tsp grated fresh root
   ginger
1 tsp cumin seeds
½ tsp ground coriander
¼ tsp turmeric
2 waxy potatoes, boiled
   and diced
1 tsp salt

Cut stalk from the cauliflower and break the head into small florets.

Heat the oil in a non-stick frying pan. Add the cauliflower florets and fry briskly for 2-3 minutes, then transfer to a plate using a slotted spoon.

Add the onion, garlic and ginger to the pan and fry over moderately high heat until lightly browned. Add the cumin and fry for a few seconds, then stir in the coriander and turmeric. Pour in 2 fl oz/50ml water, then add the potatoes, fried cauliflower and the salt.

Cover and cook gently for about 10 minutes, or until the cauliflower is just tender. Serve at once. **Serves 4**

MOONG DAL

Bring the beans to the boil, then drain. Bring to the boil in fresh water and drain. Return to the pan and cover with fresh water. Bring to the boil, cover and simmer very gently for 35-40 minutes, until tender. Remove from the heat.

Heat the oil in a frying pan. Add the onion and fry gently for 2 minutes. Stir in the garlic and ginger and cook for 1 minute, then stir in the turmeric. Add the carrots and cook, stirring, for about 3 minutes, until just tender. Add the cabbage and cook, stirring, for 3 minutes. Pour in 2fl oz/50ml water.

Drain the beans and add to the pan. Cook gently, stirring, for 2 minutes. Season to taste. Serve at once.

Serves 4-6

*6oz/175g moong beans,
  rinsed and soaked
  overnight in cold water*
4tbls oil
1 onion, chopped
2 garlic cloves, chopped
*1 tsp grated fresh root
  ginger*
2tsp turmeric
2 carrots, finely chopped
*4oz/100g cabbage,
  shredded*
1 tbls lemon juice
salt

POTATO PATTIES

1lb/450g floury potatoes,
  sliced
salt
4oz/100g frozen peas
8tbls oil
1 small onion, chopped
1 green chilli, seeded and
  chopped
1tsp grated fresh root
  ginger
1tbls plain flour
¼tsp turmeric
For the coating:
1 egg
3oz/75g fresh
  breadcrumbs

Cook the potatoes in boiling salted water for 10 minutes. Add the peas and continue cooking until the potatoes are tender. Drain well and mash.

Heat 2tbls oil in a frying pan. Add the onion and cook until soft but not brown. Add the chilli and ginger and cook, stirring, for 1 minute. Sprinkle in the flour and turmeric and cook for 30 seconds. Stir in the mashed potato mixture and salt, to taste. Mix thoroughly, then spoon the mixture on to a plate. Leave to cool, then cover and chill for at least 30 minutes.

Divide the mixture into 8 equal portions and shape each into a pattie.

Beat the egg with 1tbls water. Spread the breadcrumbs on a plate. Dip each pattie in egg and then in breadcrumbs.

Fry the patties, 2 or 3 at a time, in the remaining oil, for about 4 minutes on each side until browned. Drain on absorbent paper and keep warm while frying the remainder.

Serve at once. **Serves 4**

HOT BEETROOT RELISH

Heat the oil in a saucepan. Add the onion and fry until lightly coloured. Stir in the garlic and cumin. Pour in the tomatoes and cook over moderately high heat for 2-3 minutes. Add the vinegar and salt, then stir in the beetroot and simmer for 4 minutes.

Spoon into a warmed serving dish, sprinkle with coriander, if liked, and serve at once. **Serves 4-6**

3tbls oil
1 onion, chopped
1 garlic clove, chopped
2tsp ground cumin
14oz/400g can chopped tomatoes
1tsp malt vinegar
½tsp salt
12oz/350g cooked beetroot, cut into large cubes
chopped coriander leaves, to garnish (optional)

CARROT DESSERT

1lb/450g carrots, coarsely
  grated
8 cardamom pods
1in/2.5cm piece cinnamon
  stick
1 pint/600ml milk
2tbls oil
2oz/50g unsalted butter
1½oz/40g caster sugar
1tbls sultanas
1tbls unsalted shelled
  pistachios

Place the carrots in a large non-stick
frying pan with the cardamom and
cinnamon. Pour in the milk. Simmer
gently for about 45 minutes, stirring
occasionally, until the carrots have
absorbed the milk.

Transfer the carrots to a dish. Clean
and dry the pan.

Heat the oil and butter in the pan.
When the butter has melted, add the
carrots. Cook gently, stirring
constantly, for 10-15 minutes, until the
carrots no longer look wet. Add the
sugar and cook, stirring, for a further
2 minutes. Stir in the sultanas and the
pistachios.

Spoon the mixture into a serving
bowl and leave to cool. Serve cold.
Serves 4

KULFI

Lightly crush the cardamom pods, then place in a saucepan with one-quarter of the evaporated milk. Heat gently until warm, then remove from the heat. Cover and leave to infuse for 20 minutes.

Strain the flavoured milk into a mixing bowl. Stir in remaining evaporated milk, the caster sugar, almonds, rose water and cream. Pour into a freezerproof container, cover and freeze for 2 hours, or until slushy. Turn into a bowl and whisk until smooth. Return to the container, cover and freeze for a further 1 hour. Whisk once again, then freeze until almost firm.

Stir the ice cream, then pour into a 1½ pint/850ml freezerproof pudding basin lined with cling film. Cover and freeze for about 4 hours, until firm.

Transfer the basin to the refrigerator about 1 hour before serving to allow the ice cream to soften. When ready to serve, slip a palette knife between the sides of the basin and cling film and run around the sides to loosen the ice cream. Turn out the ice cream on to a serving dish and peel off the cling film.

Decorate with petals, if liked, and serve at once. **Serves 8**

10 cardamom pods
2 x 14oz/400g cans
  evaporated milk
4tbls caster sugar
2oz/50g blanched
  almonds, chopped
1tbls rose water
¼ pint/150ml double
  cream
flower petals, to decorate
  (optional)

LIMEADE

3 large limes
1 ½oz/40g caster sugar
To garnish:
lime slices
sprigs of mint

Thinly pare the zest from the limes in long strips. Place the strips in a heatproof jug with the sugar. Pour in 1 pint/600ml boiling water and stir well, then cover and leave to cool.

Remove and discard the strips of zest. Squeeze the juice from the limes and add to the jug. Dilute with cold water to taste, then cover and chill for at least 1 hour.

To serve, pour into a jug or chilled glasses and garnish with lime slices and mint sprigs. **Makes about 1 ¼ pints/ 700ml**

SAFFRON SWEETMEAT

½ pint/300ml milk
6 cardamom pods
¼tsp freshly grated nutmeg
½tsp saffron strands, ground (see p5)
2 eggs
2 egg yolks
2oz/50g caster sugar
2oz/50g butter, melted
2oz/50g ground almonds
1tbls rose water
flaked almonds, cut into slivers, to decorate

Pour the milk into a small saucepan. Add the cardamom and nutmeg. Heat gently until warm, then remove from the heat. Cover and leave to infuse for 20 minutes, then strain.

Pour 3tbls hot water over the saffron and set aside.

Beat the eggs, egg yolks and sugar together with a wooden spoon, then slowly stir in the strained milk. Stir in the melted butter, almonds, rose water and saffron liquid.

Pour into a well buttered 1in/2.5cm deep, 7in/18cm square baking tin. Bake in the oven preheated to 325F/160C/ Gas 3 for 30-40 minutes until shrunken from the sides of the tin and set in the centre. Leave to cool in the tin.

To serve, cut the mixture into 1in/ 2.5cm squares. Carefully remove the squares from the tin and decorate with a sliver of almond. Any left over sweetmeats will keep in an airtight container in the refrigerator for 2-3 days. **Makes 36 squares**

MEDITERRANEAN AND MIDDLE EAST

AUBERGINE PÂTÉ

2 aubergines
2 garlic cloves, crushed
1 tsp lemon juice
2 tbls light tahini
1 tbls olive oil
1 tbls chopped parsley
salt and black pepper
warmed pitta bread, cut
  into strips, to serve

Cut the aubergines in half lengthways and place, cut side down, on a baking sheet. Bake in the oven preheated to 400F/200C/Gas 6 for about 30 minutes, until the skins are lightly charred and the flesh is soft when pierced with a knife.

Using a spoon, scoop the aubergine flesh into a bowl. Discard the skins. Using a fork, stir in the garlic, lemon juice, tahini, oil and parsley. Season to taste, then cover and chill for at least 2 hours.

Serve with pitta bread. **Serves 4**

FALAFEL

2 x 15oz/425g cans chick-
  peas, drained and
  rinsed
1 Spanish onion, finely
  chopped
4 spring onions, thinly
  sliced
1 tbls coriander leaves,
  chopped
2 garlic cloves, crushed
1/2 tsp cayenne pepper
1/2 tsp ground cumin
1 tbls plain flour
pinch of salt
oil, for deep frying
To serve:
small lettuce leaves
warmed pitta bread
lemon wedges

Mash the chick-peas with a potato ricer or in a food processor. Place in a mixing bowl with the onions, coriander, garlic, cayenne, cumin, flour and salt. Mix together well.

Divide the mixture into walnut-size pieces and roll each into a small ball on a floured surface. Chill for about 30 minutes, to firm.

Heat the oil in a deep-fat frier to 370F/180C. Fry the falafels, a few at a time, for about 3 minutes until golden. Drain on absorbent paper and keep warm while you fry the remaining falafels.

Serve the falafels on a bed of lettuce leaves, and accompanied by pitta bread and lemon wedges. **Serves 4-6**

STUFFED PEPPERS

6 even-sized red or green
   peppers
For the filling:
2tbls oil
1 onion, chopped
1 garlic clove, crushed
2oz/50g long grain rice
1lb/450g minced beef
14oz/400g can chopped
   tomatoes
1/2tsp freshly grated
   nutmeg
2tbls chopped coriander
   leaves
salt and black pepper
For the topping:
2tbls fresh brown
   breadcrumbs
1oz/25g butter, melted

Cut the tops off the peppers and reserve as 'lids'. Remove the seeds and membrane.

Place the pepper and lids in a large pan. Cover with water and bring to the boil, then drain and rinse under cold running water. Cut a sliver from the base of each pepper, if necessary, so they will stand upright, then place in an ovenproof dish. Remove the stalks from some of the lids.

Make the filling: heat the oil in a saucepan. Add the onion and cook until softened. Add the garlic and rice and fry for 1-2 minutes. Stir in the mince and fry until browned. Add the tomatoes, nutmeg and coriander and season to taste. Cover and cook for 15-20 minutes, then remove from the heat.

Divide the filling between the peppers. Mix the breadcrumbs and butter and sprinkle over the filling. Replace the lids. Pour a little water into the dish around the peppers. Bake in the oven preheated to 350F/180C/Gas 4 for 40-50 minutes until the peppers are tender. Serve hot or cold. **Serves 6**

PORTUGUESE SARDINES

Using the back of a sharp knife and working from the tail to the head, scrape the sardines under cold running water to remove the scales. Slit the belly open, remove the entrails and rinse clean. Make 2 small slashes on each side. Place fish on grill rack.

Make the sauce: heat the oil in a saucepan. Add the onion and garlic and fry until softened. Stir in the tomato purée and tomatoes and simmer gently for 10-15 minutes, until thickened. Stir in the basil and season to taste.

Meanwhile, cook the sardines under a moderate grill for about 10 minutes, turning once, until the flesh flakes easily when tested with a fork.

Garnish and serve, with the sauce.

Serves 4

1lb/450g sardines
basil sprigs, to garnish
For the sauce:
2tbls oil
1 onion, chopped
2 garlic cloves, crushed
2tbls tomato purée
1lb/450g tomatoes, chopped
1tbls fresh basil, chopped
salt and black pepper

ISRAELI CARROT SALAD

4oz/100g carrots,
  coarsely grated
juice of 1 orange
1 tbls lemon juice
1 orange
2 avocados
1 tbls olive oil
pinch of ground ginger
a little caster sugar

Place the carrots in a bowl and sprinkle with the orange and lemon juice. Cover and leave for 1 hour.

Peel the orange, removing all the bitter white pith. Cut between the membrane with a sharp knife to free the segments. Remove any pips and cut the segments in half. Stir the segments into the carrots. Halve and stone the avocados. Brush the cut surfaces with a little of the lemon and orange juice drained from the carrots to prevent browning.

Mix the oil with the ginger and sugar, to taste, then sprinkle over the grated carrots. Stir well to mix, then divide the mixture between the avocados. **Serves 4**

PASTA WITH HERBS

8oz/225g long vermicelli
  or spaghetti
salt
4 tbls olive oil
3 garlic cloves, chopped
3 tbls chopped marjoram
  or 1 tbls dried marjoram
2 tbls chopped parsley
1 tbls lemon juice
knob of butter
black pepper
grated Parmesan cheese,
  to serve

Cook the pasta in plenty of boiling salted water until just tender. Drain well and keep hot.

Heat the oil in a large saucepan. Add the garlic and fry gently for 1 minute. Stir in the marjoram, parsley and lemon juice. Add the drained pasta and butter. Stir round with a wooden fork to mix thoroughly, seasoning to taste.

Turn into a warmed serving dish and sprinkle with Parmesan cheese. Serve at once, with more cheese handed separately, if liked. **Serves 2-4**

GARLIC MUSHROOMS

Cut the mushrooms into quarters.

Make the garlic mayonnaise: place the mayonnaise in a bowl and stir in the garlic and lemon juice. Season to taste and thin slightly with milk.

Add the mushrooms to the garlic mayonnaise and mix gently until evenly coated. Cover and chill for at least 2 hours.

To serve, turn the mushrooms into a serving bowl or 4 individual dishes. Dust with paprika and garnish.
Serves 4

8oz/225g button
  mushrooms
sweet paprika, for dusting
lettuce leaves, to garnish
**For the garlic
  mayonnaise:**
¼ pint/150ml mayonnaise
2 garlic cloves, crushed
1 tbls lemon juice
salt and black pepper
1-2 tbls milk

ITALIAN SWEETBREADS

1lb/450g calf's
   sweetbreads
salt
1tbls lemon juice
1oz/25g unsalted butter
1tbls oil
4oz/100g rindless lean
   bacon rashers, thinly
   sliced
2tbls chopped sage, or
   1tsp dried sage
3tbls Marsala or Madeira
black pepper
boiled rice, to serve

Cover the sweetbreads with cold water and leave to soak for 1 hour, then drain. Place in a saucepan with cold water to cover, 1tsp salt and the lemon juice. Bring slowly to the boil, then drain. Leave in fresh cold water until cool enough to handle, then remove the membrane, veins and connective tissue.

Pat the sweetbreads dry on absorbent paper and cut into slices.

Melt the butter with the oil in a frying pan. Add the sweetbreads and fry fairly briskly until light golden, then transfer to a plate. Add the bacon and the sage to the pan and fry for about 3 minutes. Add the wine and cook, stirring, until syrupy.

Return the sweetbreads to the pan, season to taste and heat through.

Serve at once, with rice. **Serves 3-4**

SPANISH KIDNEYS

3tbls oil
1 Spanish onion, chopped
2 garlic cloves, chopped
1lb/450g calf's or lamb's
   kidneys, skinned, sliced
   and cored
1tbls plain flour
3fl oz/85ml dry sherry
1/2 pint/300ml beef or
   chicken stock
1tbls tomato purée
2 bay leaves
salt and black pepper
boiled rice, to serve

Heat the oil in a frying pan, add the onion and garlic and fry until soft but not brown. Add the kidneys and cook for 2-3 minutes until lightly browned.

Sprinkle in the flour and cook, stirring, for 1 minute. Pour in the sherry and cook, stirring, for 2 minutes, then gradually stir in the stock and tomato purée. Add 1 bay leaf and season to taste. Cook gently, stirring, for about 2 minutes, or until the kidneys are tender. Remove the bay leaf and check the seasoning.

Spoon the kidneys on to a bed or ring of boiled rice, garnish with the remaining bay leaf and serve at once. **Serves 4**

ARABIAN LAMB CASSEROLE

1oz/25g butter
1tbls oil
1 large onion, sliced
1¼lb/500g neck of lamb
   fillet, cut into 1in/
   2.5cm cubes
1tbls plain flour
½ pint/300ml lamb stock
salt and black pepper
4oz/100g dried prunes,
   soaked overnight,
   drained and stoned, or
   ready to eat tenderized
   prunes
2oz/50g no-need-to-soak
   dried apricots
1oz/25g blanched
   almonds
1tbls lemon juice
1tbls granulated sugar

Melt the butter with the oil in a large flameproof casserole. Add the onion and fry until lightly browned. Add the lamb and fry over high heat until browned on all sides.

Stir in the flour, then gradually stir in the stock. Season to taste, then cover and simmer gently for 45 minutes.

Add the prunes, apricots, almonds, lemon juice and sugar. Cover and cook gently for 20-30 minutes, until the meat and fruit are tender. Check the seasoning and serve. **Serves 4**

TURKISH ROAST DUCK

Trim off excess fat from the duck, reserving 2tbls fat for the sauce.

Make the stuffing: heat the oil in a saucepan. Add the onion and fry until softened. Remove from the heat and stir in the apple, orange zest, 2oz/50g raisins, the nuts, spice, rice and salt.

Spoon the stuffing into the duck. Place the duck on a rack in a roasting tin and prick the skin well with a sharp fork. Roast the duck in the oven preheated to 400F/200C/Gas 6 for 1½ hours, basting occasionally.

Meanwhile, place the giblets in saucepan with 1 pint/600ml water. Simmer for 1 hour, then strain. Measure out ½ pint/300ml stock.

Sift flour over duck. Increase heat to 425F/220C/Gas 7 and roast duck for a further 10 minutes, or until the juices run clear when tested with a fork.

Make the sauce: melt the reserved duck fat in a small saucepan. Stir in the flour, then the measured stock. Simmer for 1 minute, then stir in the orange juice, tomato purée, butter and remaining raisins.

Transfer duck to a serving dish and pour over the sauce. Garnish and serve.
Serves 4

4lb/1.75kg oven-ready duck, defrosted if frozen, giblets reserved
1tbls plain flour, for dredging
parsley sprigs, to garnish
For the stuffing:
2tbls oil
4oz/100g onion, chopped
1 dessert apple, quartered, cored and chopped
grated zest of ½ orange
4oz/100g seedless raisins
1oz/25g pine nuts or chopped blanched almonds
pinch of ground mixed spice
8oz/225g boiled rice
large pinch salt
For the sauce:
2tbls plain flour
juice of 1½ oranges
1tsp tomato purée
knob of butter

VEAL ESPAGNOLE

1½lb/700g lean veal, cut
   into 1in/2.5cm cubes
1oz/25g plain flour
2tbls oil
3oz/75g unsmoked
   gammon slice, rind
   removed, cut into
   ½in/1cm cubes
1 onion, chopped
2 garlic cloves, crushed
½oz/15g unsalted butter
¼ pint/150ml dry white
   wine
2 chillies, seeded and
   sliced
1 celery stalk, thinly
   sliced
1tbls tomato purée
½ pint/300ml chicken
   stock
salt
4oz/100g frozen or shelled
   fresh peas
boiled rice or noodles,
   sprinkled with chopped
   parsley, to serve

Turn the veal cubes in the flour until
evenly coated and reserve.

Heat the oil in a flameproof
casserole. Add the gammon, onion and
garlic and fry until coloured. Remove
from the pan with a slotted spoon.

Melt the butter in the pan, add the
veal cubes and fry, stirring, until
browned on all sides. Pour in the wine
and simmer until reduced by about half.

Return the gammon and onion
mixture to the pan. Stir in the chillies,
celery, tomato purée and stock and
season with salt. Bring to the boil, then
cover, lower the heat and simmer
gently for 1½ hours. Add the peas and
cook for a further 5 minutes or until the
veal is tender and the peas are cooked.

Serve from the casserole,
accompanied by rice or noodles.

Serves 4-6

GALACIAN PORK

Place the pork in a saucepan and fry gently until the fat begins to run. Add the gammon knuckle, chicken joint and onions. Pour in 2 pints/1.2 litres water, bring to the boil and skim the scum from the surface. Add the leek and carrots, cover and cook gently for 1½ hours.

Add the potatoes and cabbage to the pan with the chorizos and black pudding. Cover and cook gently for a further 15-20 minutes, until potato is tender.

Using a slotted spoon, remove the meat, sausages and vegetables from the pan. Take the meat off the bones and cut it into chunks. Slice the vegetables. Divide the meat, sausages and vegetables between 4-6 warmed serving bowls. Ladle the stock from the pan into the bowls and serve at once.

Serves 4-6

*12oz/350g lean belly of
  pork, cut into 2in/5cm
  chunks*
1 gammon knuckle
1 chicken quarter
2 onions
*1 large leek, cut across in
  half*
2 carrots
2 waxy potatoes, diced
*8oz/225g cabbage,
  shredded*
3 chorizos, thickly sliced
*4oz/100g black pudding,
  thickly sliced*

LAMB PILAF

3tbls oil
1 large onion, chopped
1lb/450g neck of lamb
    fillet, cut into 1in/
    2.5cm cubes
2oz/50g pine nuts or
    chopped blanched
    almonds
1oz/25g sultanas
½tsp ground cinnamon
½tsp freshly grated
    nutmeg
3tbls tomato purée
salt and black pepper
1 pint/600ml lamb stock
6oz/175g long grain rice
bay leaves, to garnish
natural yoghurt, to serve
    (optional)

Heat the oil in a large saucepan. Add the onion and fry until lightly browned. Add the lamb and cook, stirring, until lightly browned on all sides.

Add the nuts and stir until coloured, then stir in the sultanas, cinnamon, nutmeg and tomato purée. Season to taste.

Pour in the stock, cover and simmer gently, stirring occasionally, for 40 minutes. Stir in the rice and bring to the boil. Lower the heat, cover and cook gently for 15-20 minutes until all the liquid has been absorbed and the rice is tender. Check the rice towards the end of cooking time and add a little water, if necessary, to prevent the pilaf drying out.

Spoon the pilaf on to warmed serving plates. Garnish each portion with a bay leaf. Serve at once, with yoghurt, if liked. **Serves 4-6**

GREEK MACARONI BAKE

Heat the oil in a frying pan. Add the onions and fry until lightly browned. Add the mince and cook, stirring, until browned. Stir in the tomato purée, a little salt, the garlic and marjoram. Cook, stirring frequently, for 10 minutes. Remove from the heat.

Meanwhile, cook the macaroni in plenty of boiling salted water for about 10 minutes, until just tender. Drain the macaroni, then spread over the base of 4 small greased gratin dishes or 1 large greased ovenproof dish.

Make the sauce: melt the margarine in a saucepan. Add the flour and cook, stirring, for 1 minute, then gradually stir in the milk. Add the nutmeg and season to taste. Remove from heat.

Spoon one-third of the sauce over the macaroni. Spread the mince mixture over the top, then cover with the remaining sauce. Sprinkle the grated cheese over the top.

Bake in the oven preheated to 375F/ 190C/Gas 5 for 40-45 minutes, until golden brown. Serve hot, with salad.

Serves 4

2 tbls oil
2 onions, finely chopped
1 lb/450g minced beef or lamb
3 tbls tomato purée
salt
1 garlic clove, crushed
½ tsp chopped marjoram, or ¼ tsp dried marjoram
8 oz/225g long macaroni or rigatoni
½ oz/15g Cheddar cheese, grated
small green salad, to serve
For the sauce:
½ oz/15g margarine or butter
½ oz/15g plain flour
1 pint/600ml warm milk
¼ tsp freshly grated nutmeg
black pepper

PERSIAN OMELETTE

2tbls oil
1 large onion, chopped
12oz/350g minced beef or
    lamb
1 waxy potato, coarsely
    grated
½tsp ground coriander
1tsp ground cumin
3tbls chopped parsley
salt and black pepper
4 eggs, well beaten
parsley sprig, to garnish

Heat the oil in a heavy-based frying pan. Add the onion and fry until golden. Add the mince and cook, stirring, until browned.

Stir in the potato, coriander, cumin and chopped parsley. Season to taste. Cook, stirring, for about 5 minutes, until the potato is tender.

Pour in the eggs and stir until evenly mixed. Cover the pan and cook very gently for 10-15 minutes, until the omelette is set underneath.

Uncover the pan and place under a medium grill. Cook for 5 minutes, until the surface of the omelette is set and lightly browned. Turn the pan around frequently to ensure even browning and take care the handle does not scorch.

Slide the omelette on to a serving dish and garnish with parsley. Serve hot or cold, cut into wedges. **Serves 4**

FOIL-BAKED MACKEREL

salt and black pepper
4 mackerel, cleaned
2tbls oil
1 large onion, chopped
3 celery stalks, thinly
    sliced
1 garlic clove, crushed
2tbls chopped parsley
1tsp dillweed
1tbls lemon juice

Season the cavity of each mackerel, then place each fish on a piece of foil large enough to enclose it.

Heat the oil in a frying pan. Add the onion and celery and fry gently until soft but not brown. Stir in the garlic, parsley, dillweed and lemon juice. Season to taste. Remove from the heat.

Spoon one-quarter of the mixture over each fish. Wrap the fish loosely in the foil, crimping the edges to seal. Place the fish parcels on a baking sheet. Bake in the oven preheated to 375F/ 190C/Gas 5 for 25-30 minutes, until the flesh flakes easily when tested with a fork.

Transfer each fish, in its foil wrapping, to a warmed serving plate. Serve at once. **Serves 4**

SEAFOOD SALAD

6oz/175g salmon steak
8oz/225g haddock or cod
steak
2 squid, cleaned and
sliced (optional)
2 shelled and cleaned
fresh or frozen scallops
1 bouquet garni
2tbls lemon juice
5oz/150g cooked mussels
in brine, drained
4-6 cooked King prawns
fennel sprigs, to garnish
For the dressing:
3tbls oil
2tbls chopped mixed herbs
or 1tbls dried mixed
herbs
salt and black pepper

Place the salmon, haddock, squid (if using) and scallops in a large saucepan. Add the bouquet garni, 1tbls lemon juice and water to just cover. Bring slowly to simmering point, then cover and simmer very gently for about 10 minutes, until the fish flakes easily when tested with a fork. Remove from the heat.

Transfer the fish, scallops and squid to a plate with a slotted spoon. Remove the skin and bones from the fish and flake the flesh into even-sized pieces. Slice the scallops. Divide the flaked fish, squid, scallops and mussels between 4-6 individual serving plates. Arrange a prawn on each plate.

To make the dressing, place the oil in a small bowl with the remaining lemon juice and the herbs. Season to taste, then whisk together with a fork until blended.

Pour the dressing over the salads and garnish with fennel. **Serves 4-6**

MEDITERRANEAN FISH SOUP

Place the vegetables and garlic cloves in a large saucepan. Add the fish, orange zest, bouquet garni and a little salt. Pour in 2 pints/1.2 litres water. Cover and simmer gently for about 10 minutes, until the fish flakes easily.

Transfer the fish and potatoes to a dish and keep warm.

Boil the cooking liquid until reduced to about 1 pint/600ml. Remove from the heat, check seasoning and strain.

Place half the garlic mayonnaise in a saucepan. Stir in the reduced stock.

Divide the toast between 4-6 serving bowls. Top with the fish and potatoes. Re-heat the stock mixture, without boiling, then pour over the fish. Serve at once, with the remaining mayonnaise. **Serves 4-6**

1 large onion, chopped
1 leek, sliced
2 small tomatoes
2 large waxy potatoes, thinly sliced
2 garlic cloves, crushed
1½lb/700g firm white fish fillets, skinned and cut into large pieces
2 strips orange zest
1 bouquet garni
salt and black pepper
¼ pint/150ml garlic mayonnaise (see p79)
8-12 thin slices French bread, toasted, rubbed with garlic and sprinkled with olive oil

VEGETABLES AU GRATIN

2 aubergines, cut into
  ½in/1cm slices
salt
2fl oz/50ml oil
1 large onion, chopped
2 garlic cloves, crushed
12oz/350g courgettes,
  sliced
2 beef tomatoes, sliced
1tsp chopped summer
  savory or mixed herbs
black pepper
For the topping:
3oz/75g Cheddar cheese,
  grated
¼ pint/150ml natural
  yoghurt

Place the aubergines in a colander, sprinkling the layers with salt. Leave for 30 minutes, then rinse and dry.

Heat the oil in a large frying pan. Fry the aubergines, in batches, until lightly browned on both sides. Drain on absorbent paper and reserve.

Add the onion and garlic to the pan and fry until softened. Add the courgettes and cook, stirring, for 2-3 minutes. Remove from the heat.

Arrange half the aubergines in the base of 4 individual gratin dishes or a large shallow ovenproof dish. Top with the courgette mixture and tomatoes. Sprinkle over the herbs and season to taste. Add remaining aubergines.

Stir the cheese into the yoghurt and spoon evenly over the vegetables. Bake in the oven preheated to 375F/190C/ Gas 5 for 30-40 minutes, until the topping is golden and the aubergines are tender. Serve hot or cold.
Serves 4-6

ITALIAN COURGETTES

1lb/450g courgettes,
  coarsely grated
salt
6tbls olive oil
1lb/450g carrots, coarsely
  grated
1tbls lemon juice
1tbls chopped chives
1tbls chopped parsley
black pepper

Line a colander with muslin or a clean tea-towel. Place the courgettes in the lined colander, sprinkle with 1tsp salt and leave to drain for 1 hour.

Wrap the courgettes in the muslin and squeeze to extract as much liquid as possible. Tip the courgettes on to absorbent paper and reserve.

Heat the oil in a large non-stick frying pan. Add the carrots and cook over a moderate heat for 5 minutes, stirring occasionally. Add the courgettes and continue to cook, stirring, until tender. Sprinkle with the lemon juice and herbs and season to taste. Serve at once. **Serves 4-6**

FRENCH BAKED POTATOES

Cover the potatoes with cold water and leave to soak for 15 minutes, then drain and dry on absorbent paper.

Rub the inside of 6 individual gratin dishes or 1 large shallow ovenproof dish with garlic. Sprinkle in a little oil.

Layer the potatoes in the dishes, seasoning each layer and sprinkling with oil and herbs. Slowly pour in the stock.

Bake in the oven preheated to 400F/200C/Gas 6 for 1½ hours, or until the potatoes are tender. **Serves 6**

*2lb/1kg waxy potatoes,
  thinly sliced
1 garlic clove
4tbls olive oil
salt and black pepper
2tsp chopped rosemary
2tsp chopped thyme
½ pint/300ml vegetable
  stock*

WATERMELON COOLER

3¼lb/1.5kg wedge
watermelon
1oz/25g caster sugar
1tbls lemon juice
To garnish:
lemon slices
mint sprigs

Remove the rind from the watermelon, then cut the flesh into chunks. Scrape out the seeds with a fork.

Purée the watermelon flesh with the sugar, in batches if necessary, in a blender or food processor. Strain the purée into a jug and stir in the lemon juice. Cover and chill for at least 2 hours.

To serve, pour into tall glasses and garnish with a lemon slice and mint.
Serves 4-6

FLUFFY ZABAGLIONE

3 egg yolks
3oz/75g caster sugar
6tbls Marsala
1 egg white
grated chocolate, to
decorate
sponge finger biscuits, to
serve

Place the egg yolks and sugar in a large heat-proof bowl. Set over a pan of gently simmering water and whisk until the egg yolks begin to thicken. Add the Marsala and continue whisking for about 5-10 minutes, or until the mixture can hold soft peaks.

Remove the bowl from the pan and continue whisking for a few minutes until the mixture is cool.

Using clean beaters, whisk the egg white until stiff. Fold the egg white into the egg yolk mixture.

Spoon the mixture into dessert glasses or dishes. Sprinkle with grated chocolate and serve at once, with biscuits. **Serves 4-6**

GREEK YOGHURT DESSERT

¾ pint/450ml thick
natural yoghurt
3tbls clear honey
2oz/50g blanched
almonds, toasted and
chopped
ground cinnamon, for
dusting

Drain any liquid from the yoghurt, then turn into a bowl. Stir in the honey and nuts. Divide between individual dessert glasses or dishes, cover and chill until ready to serve.

Just before serving, sprinkle each dessert with cinnamon. **Serves 2-4**

INDEX